IT'S AMAZING!
PIRATES

Annabel Savery

A⁺
Smart Apple Media

Published by Smart Apple Media, an imprint of Black Rabbit Books
P.O. Box 3263, Mankato, Minnesota 56002
www.blackrabbitbooks.com

Printed in the United States of America at Corporate Graphics, North Mankato, Minnesota.

Published by arrangement with the Watts Publishing Group LTD, London.

Library of Congress Cataloging-in-Publication Data
Savery, Annabel.
Pirates / Annabel Savery.
p. cm.—(It's amazing!)
Includes index.
Summary: "Describes the daily lives and traits of pirates from around the world.
Also highlights famous pirates in history as well as from books and movies"
—Provided by publisher.
ISBN 978-1-59920-690-5 (library binding)
1. Pirates—Juvenile literature. I. Title.
G535.S28 2013
910.4'5—dc23

2011033717

Planning and production by Discovery Books Limited
Managing editor: Laura Durman
Editor: Annabel Savery
Designer: Ian Winton

Picture credits: Alamy: p. 19 top & p. 24 bottom (North Wind Picture Archives), p. 28 bottom (Moviestore Collection Limited), p. 29 top (AF Archive); Corbis: p. 7 (Richard T Nowitz); Getty Images: p. 5 , p. 13 top, p. 16 & p.31 (all Candela Foto Art/Kreuziger), p. 21 (Ambroise-Louis Garneray), p. 23 top (James Edwin McConnell), p. 27 top (Hulton Archive/Stringer), p. 27 top (Apic/Contributor); iStockPhoto.com : p. 20 bottom (duncan1890); Photoshot: p. 29 bottom; Rex Features: p. 28 top; Shutterstock Images: title & p. 12 (Bobby Deal/RealDealPhoto), p. 4 & p. 6 (RCPPHOTO), p. 7 top (Harry H Marsh), p. 8 (pgaborphotos), p. 11 top (Sakala), p. 11 bottom (Tracy Whiteside), p. 13 bottom (Oxana Zuboff), p. 14 (Aaron Whitney), p. 15 top (Andreas Meyer), p. 15 bottom (Eric Isselée), p. 18 (Dwight Smith), p. 19 top (Elena Schweitzer), p. 22 main (Paul B Moore), p. 24 top (Alexander Smulskiy); Wikimedia Commons: p. 9 top, p. 9 bottom, p. 10, p. 17 top, p. 20 top, p. 22 inset, p. 23 bottom, p. 25, p. 26 top, p. 26 bottom.
Cover credit: Shutterstock Images (Bobby Deal/RealDealPhoto)

Please note that due to the subject matter of this book many of the photographs are reconstructions.

PO1434 / 2-2012

9 8 7 6 5 4 3 2 1

CONTENTS

All words in **bold** appear in the glossary on page 30.

DASTARDLY PIRATES!

Imagine sailing on the high seas with valuable **cargo** of gold and silver. Suddenly, you see another ship on the **horizon**. Through your telescope you can see the flag on top of its **mast**. Pirates!

Ever since people began **transporting** cargo on the seas, pirates have sailed too. They would try to steal the valuable cargo.

Pirates would steal anything, from precious metals and jewels, to food, clothes, and weapons. They were fierce and bloodthirsty, often taking sailors prisoner or killing them.

Pirates Today

Pirates are still around today and are very dangerous. Modern pirates may look different from **traditional** pirates, but they still steal anything, from animals to weapons. They sometimes even take people **hostage** so that they can demand a **ransom** from them.

PIRATE SHIPS

Every pirate has a pirate ship to sail across the oceans looking for treasure.

Before **engines** were invented, ships had sails and were powered by the wind. When there was no wind, pirates had to row the ship using long **oars**.

Pirate ships like this one were small and fast. Cargo ships were heavy and slow.

Mast

Sail

Pirate ships could sail quickly up to cargo ships to attack them. Both ships had cannons and there were fierce battles whenever the two met.

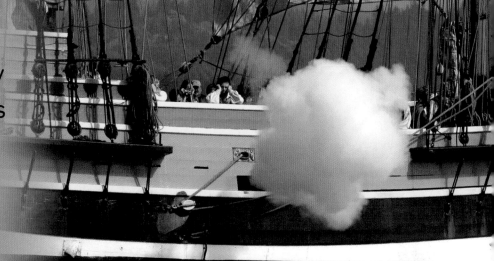

IT'S AMAZING!

We know lots about pirates from shipwrecks that have been found. Divers (below) have even found some pirate ships with stolen treasure still aboard.

THE JOLLY ROGER

How did sailors know when a ship belonged to pirates? Because it was flying a Jolly Roger!

The Jolly Roger is the pirate flag. It was usually a black flag with a picture of a skull and crossbones on it, like the one above.

But many pirates had their own flag design. It usually showed something to do with death, such as a skeleton having a drink with a sailor.

Red Flags

Not all pirate flags were black and white. Sailors were very scared of a pirate ship with a red flag, as this meant the pirates on board would kill everyone they could in a battle!

PIRATE STYLE

Pirates often had very good clothing because they stole it from the crew of the ships that they plundered.

The pirate captain often had the fanciest clothes. When rich **merchant** ships were robbed, the pirate captain would take all of the best things for himself.

Many pirates liked to wear tricorne hats like this. These were made of leather and had three corners. Captain Jack Sparrow wears a hat like this in the *Pirates of the Caribbean* movies.

Tricorne hat

Pirates also wore bandanas. These were brightly colored pieces of cloth that were tied around the head.

Bandana

Bejeweled Pirates!

Pirates often wore lots of jewelry. This showed others how good they were at stealing!

PIRATE WEAPONS

Pirates were always well armed so that they could attack ships at a moment's notice.

Pistol

Cutlass

Most pirate weapons were stolen from the ships that they plundered.

Over time, weapons changed a lot. Early pirates used cutlasses. These were swords with sharp, curved blades.

Later, pirates used guns called pistols and muskets as well (right).

Some pirates even used axes. These could be used to climb the sides of a wooden ship. On board, an axe would be used to cut the ropes holding the sails up and to attack people.

Musket

Pistol

IT'S AMAZING!

Gunpowder was kept on all ships and was used to fire guns and cannons (below). On pirate Henry Morgan's (see page 26) ship, some drunken sailors accidentally lit a gunpowder barrel and made it explode!

LIFE ON BOARD

Pirate battles and treasure hunts were exciting, but in between, life on board ship was pretty tough for the pirate crew.

Pirates had to do chores to keep the ship in good shape. They would scrub the decks and climb the **rigging** to mend the sails.

Rigging

The ships were crowded and only the captains had cabins (right). The crew slept in **hammocks** in any space they could find below deck.

Pirates stayed at sea for a long time, so they needed lots of food. Sometimes, they would keep live chickens on board for eggs and fresh meat.

Rats

Unfortunately, some rats usually managed to get on board, too! They would eat the pirates' food and bring diseases on board.

PIRATES ON LAND

Pirates did not stay at sea all the time. Sometimes they needed to set foot on dry land.

Pirates were often rowdy and drunken and spent their gold on rum and **gambling**. This meant they weren't wanted in most places!

Pirates were welcome in Port Royal, Jamaica, though. The British controlled this Caribbean port and the pirates stopped the Spanish Navy from attacking it.

Often, pirates would land in a port to plunder and steal from the town's people (left).

They would rule over the town and take whatever they wanted before leaving again.

A Mutiny!

Pirates argued a lot and sometimes the crew would join together against the captain. This was called a mutiny. The crew would then leave the captain and any crew loyal to him on a desert island!

THE SPANISH MAIN

Long ago, the Spanish colonies of the Caribbean and South America were known as the Spanish Main.

When the Spanish invaded these lands, they stole gold and silver from the Aztec and Inca peoples that lived there. The Spanish took the precious metals back to Spain. It was a dangerous journey. To try to keep their cargo safe, they traveled in big **fleets** of 100 ships.

Aztec gold coin

In the fleet (below), there would be too many Spanish ships for the pirates to attack. But if any were separated from the fleet, the pirates would pounce!

Treasure Maps!

Pirate stories often tell of treasure maps that show where stolen treasure was hidden, but no maps have ever been found.

PRIVATEERS

Wars between countries were fought at sea as well as on land. One way of hurting another country was to steal the cargo that would make them richer.

Some pirates were given a "letter of marque" by the king or queen. This made them privateers.

A French letter of marque

The Queen's Pirate

One famous privateer was Sir Francis Drake (left) (1540-1596). He was given a knighthood by Queen Elizabeth I, who called him "My Pirate."

Privateers were allowed
to attack cargo ships
from other countries.
Kings and queens used
privateers to make
trade difficult
between other
countries.

In return, the privateers gave some of their
stolen treasure to the king or queen. This is the
English ship *Kent* (above) which was captured
by the French privateer Robert Surcouf in 1800.

PIRATES EVERYWHERE

Pirates came from all over the world. Wherever there was trade at sea, there were pirates.

Viking pirates sailed the seas over a thousand years ago. They came from Northern Europe, but sailed far and wide.

Vikings made very strong boats, called longboats (below). They could sail the roughest seas, but were also small enough to land close to the coasts.

A Viking helmet

The Buccaneers

The Buccaneers were a fearsome group of pirates in the 17th century. They were hunters from the island of Hispaniola (now Haiti). The Spanish forced them to leave the island, so they grouped together as pirates, attacking Spanish ships and ports.

The Barbary pirates came from the southern coast of the Mediterranean Sea. In the 16th century, they were feared all over Europe.

Pictured to the left is one of the Barbarossa brothers, two fearsome Barbary pirates.

CHINESE PIRATES

Chinese pirates were different from other pirates.

Boats called junks (right) were used by both Chinese merchants and pirates. They were small, fast ships with three triangular sails.

Chinese pirate ships worked together in battles (left) with one captain in charge.

The captain's family often lived with him on board. The pirate fleet would pass to someone in the family if the captain died.

IT'S AMAZING!

In the 18th century, pirate Zheng Yi led the biggest pirate fleet in the world, called the Red Flag Fleet. When he died, his wife Cheng Shih (above) took control of the fleet, with 1,500 boats and 60,000 pirates!

FAMOUS PIRATES

Pirates were fearsome men and women. Stories about them are still famous today.

In the 14th century, a pirate called Klaus Störtebeker terrorized the seas of northern Europe. When he was finally captured, he was **executed** along with 70 of his followers. This is a statue of him (right).

Sir Henry Morgan (left) was a ruthless pirate of the 17th century (see page 13). However, he later received a knighthood and became governor of Jamaica.

Blackbeard (left) was a terrifying 18th century pirate. He had a long, braided beard and carried six pistols. He went into battle with burning **fuses** in his hair to create a cloud of black smoke around him.

Women Pirates

Two of the most famous female pirates are Mary Read (right) and Anne Bonny. To disguise themselves, they dressed like men and were just as fearless.

PIRATE STORIES AND MOVIES

Some of the most famous pirates appear in books and movies.

Long John Silver (right) was created by Robert Louis Stevenson in his book *Treasure Island*.

IT'S AMAZING!

Treasure Island has been made into a movie five times. There is even a version (below) starring the Muppets!

Long John Silver becomes part of the crew going on a treasure hunt. He takes over the ship and tries to steal the treasure for himself!

Captain Hook is the terrible pirate of Neverland. He was created by J. M. Barrie in the book *Peter Pan*. Hook's story is also told in the movie *Hook* (right).

Pirates of the Caribbean is a series of very popular pirate movies. The stories are made up, but are based on tales of real pirates.

GLOSSARY

cargo goods carried from place to place for trade

colony a place that is under the control of another country

engine a machine that uses energy from fuel or electricity to do work

execute put to death by law

fleets groups of ships

fuse a length of material that burns easily, often used to explode a bomb or firework

gambling putting money on a certain result from a game or race

hammock a piece of material hung at both ends that people can sleep in

horizon the line where the Earth and sky appear to meet

hostage someone held as a prisoner

knighthood an award given to someone. It makes them a knight

mast a long upright pole set in the center of a ship that supports the sails

merchant a person buying and selling goods

oars long paddles that are used to move a boat through water

plunder to steal the goods from a place

ransom money demanded by kidnappers in order to free someone they have taken hostage

rigging all the ropes used on a ship to hold up the sails

shipwreck the remains of a ship that has been damaged or sunk at sea

traditional coming from the style and customs of a particular culture

transport to move things from place to place

FURTHER INFORMATION

Books

Pirates (Great Warriors), Kate Riggs, Creative Education, 2011.
Pirates (True Stories and Legends), Jim Pipe, Stargazer Books, 2010.
Pirates (Up Close), Paul Harrison, PowerKids Press, 2008.
Treasure Hunter's Handbook (Crabtree Connections), Anna Claybourne,
   Crabtree Pub. Company, 2011.

Websites

A high-seas adventure for young pirates from National Geographic.
   www.nationalgeographic.com/pirates/
Learn to talk like a pirate with this young pirates website.
   www.talklikeapirate.com/juniorpirates.html
A pirate quiz from the National Geographic Kids website.
   kids.nationalgeographic.com/kids/games/puzzlesquizzes/
   quizyournoodle-pirates/

Movies

Hook, Tristar Pictures, 1991.
Muppet Treasure Island, Buena Vista Pictures, 1996.
Treasure Island, (1950), RKO Radio Pictures, 1950.

INDEX

Note to parents and teachers: Every effort has been made by the publishers to ensure that the websites on page 31 are suitable for children, that they are of the highest educational value, and that they contain no inappropriate or offensive material. However, because of the nature of the Internet, it is impossible to guarantee that the contents of these sites will not be altered. We strongly advise that Internet access is supervised by a responsible adult.